Curriculum Visions

Sikh
faith and practice

A granthi waves the chauri.

Brian Knapp and Lisa Magloff

The Sikh faith

One must believe in certain things with mind, heart and soul; and then live by them in the course of everyday life. Faith is always personal and individual. Each person follows the faith they choose. Here are some main parts of the Sikh faith.

Sikh beliefs

▶ There is only one God, who is an omnipotent, immortal and personal Creator.

▶ The highest goals are to live truthfully, serve others selflessly and to worship only God through prayer and thinking about God.

▶ The ten Sikh Gurus are guides who were divinely inspired by God.

▶ The book called the Adi Granth, or Guru Granth Sahib, contains God's revelations and is the only source of spiritual authority.

▶ Living an honest and good life is an important part of God's will. This includes participating fully in the community, earning an honest living and treating everyone, Sikh and non-Sikh, equally.

▶ There are no castes in Sikhism and Sikhs do not believe in extremes of worship, such as fasting, celibacy and asceticism.

▶ Sikhs believe in reincarnation, that the soul is born over and over again in a new body. However, through devotion to God and living a good life, this cycle can be broken and we can achieve salvation and join with God.

▶ The goal of Sikhism is a union with God, which leads to everlasting peace and bliss.

▶ The Gurus instructed people how to live according to Sikh ideals. These include becoming baptised, wearing the five Ks and the turban, following Sikh guidelines, and always being ready to defend people who are weaker than yourself.

Find out more

Look at the companion Curriculum Visions book, 'Sikh gurdwara'.

Contents

As you go through the book, look for words in **BOLD CAPITALS**. These words are defined in the glossary.

⚠ Understanding others

Remember that other people's beliefs are important to them. You must always be considerate and understanding when studying about faith.

Sikh worship in the gurdwara.

What it means to be a Sikh

Sikhism is one of the youngest of the world religions. Sikhs believe that God is present in the heart of every person.

Sikhism was founded in the beginning of the sixteenth century by a man named **GURU NANAK DEV**. Guru Nanak lived in a region called the **PUNJAB**, in what is now modern Pakistan. The word **SIKH** comes from the Punjabi word *shishya*, which means 'a seeker of truth'.

Guru Nanak and the nine Sikh Gurus who came after him were teachers of God's word, so they are called **GURUS**, which means 'teacher'.

Sikh beliefs

Sikhs believe in one God, who is known as **WAHEGURU**, or Sat Guru ('true teacher'). God is the all-powerful Creator of the universe and Sikhs worship by praising God. The Sikh holy book, the **ADI GRANTH** or **GURU GRANTH SAHIB**, contains poems and songs in praise of God, written by people who were divinely inspired.

▶ Sikhs believe in maintaining their distinctive religious identity as well as taking a full part in society. Wearing a TURBAN is one of the requirements of a baptised Sikh, but this does not interfere with their ability to be full members of whatever society they live in. This man is a policeman. Instead of a helmet, he wears a turban.

▲ Sikhs who have been baptised have certain responsibilities, such as never to cut their hair. This Sikh man has cut his hair (notice his trimmed beard), so he has not been baptised, although he still has his Sikh faith and his belief in God and wears some of the Sikh symbols. Someday, he may decide to go through the BAPTISM ceremony.

▲ In Sikhism, baptism only takes place when a person is old enough to understand the responsibilities of being a member of the Khalsa (see pages 6 and 7). This Sikh girl is still too young to be baptised, but she worships in the gurdwara (the Sikh house of worship) and follows the Sikh faith.

Sikhism's ten Gurus each possessed the same knowledge and insight into God. Their teachings and hymns are written down in the Guru Granth Sahib. Because the Guru Granth Sahib is today considered the only Sikh spiritual leader and teacher, it is usually called simply 'The Guru'.

Like Hindus, Sikhs believe that we go through many cycles of being born, living, dying and being born again, called **REINCARNATION**, or moksha. The Gurus taught that, through devotion to God and living a good life, this cycle can be broken and we can achieve salvation and join with God.

The Sikh Gurus taught that the path to salvation could be found in the values of freedom, complete equality and tolerance, social responsibility, honest labour, living a simple life, having understanding and patience, and always being ready to help others, especially those who are weaker than ourselves.

A life of action

For Sikhs, faith is not something that only happens during worship; faith is a part of everyday life. Sikhs show their faith by taking care of their family, by working hard, by treating all people with equality and respect and by being ready to help anyone who needs it.

Maintaining ethical behaviour, sharing your earnings with the needy and working to help all of humanity are all important Sikh values.

Weblink: www.CurriculumVisions.com

The Khalsa

Anyone who follows the Sikh faith is a Sikh. But many Sikhs also go through a ceremony called **AMRIT** (baptism) in which they are welcomed into a part of Sikh society called the **KHALSA**. The word Khalsa means 'pure'. After the ceremony, men add the word Singh (lion heart) to their names, and women add the word Kaur (princess).

Sikhs who are members of the Khalsa agree to always wear the **FIVE KS**. These are: **KESH** (uncut hair), **KHANGA** (comb), **KARA** (steel bracelet), **KACCHA** (shorts) and **KIRPAN** (sword) (see pages 10 to 11). All male members of the Khalsa must also wear a turban. Women may wear a turban if they choose.

All members of the Khalsa also agree to abide by a moral and ethical code called the **REHT MARYADA**. This code applies to all Sikhs, but especially to the Khalsa. The Reht Maryada provides guidelines for every aspect of life, including how to pray and when to say certain prayers, how to conduct funeral, baptism and wedding ceremonies, and how to live according to God's will.

▶ This woman and the man opposite are members of the Khalsa, the group of baptised Sikhs. You can see the small sword at their sides, which is one of the five Ks, or symbols of the Khalsa. On the man's arm you can also clearly see the kara, steel bracelet, and he is wearing a turban, while the woman has covered her hair with a scarf. In Sikhism, men and women all have the same rights and responsibilities.

Reht Maryada

Here are some of the guidelines given in the Reht Maryada. Note that some of these only apply to members of the Khalsa.

▶ The Sikh will worship only one God. They will not set up any idols, gods, goddesses or statues for worship nor shall they worship any human being.

▶ The Sikh will believe in no religious book other than the Guru Granth Sahib, although they can study other religious books for acquiring knowledge.

▶ The Sikh will not believe in CASTES, magic, amulets, astrology, appeasement rituals, ceremonial hair cutting and fasts.

▶ The Khalsa will remain distinct by wearing the 5Ks.

▶ The Khalsa will pray to God before starting any work.

▶ A Sikh must learn PUNJABI.

▶ A Sikh woman should not wear a veil or keep her face hidden.

▶ A Sikh must live by honest labour and give generously to the poor and needy.

▶ A Sikh must never steal, gamble, drink alcohol or smoke.

▶ When a Khalsa meets another Khalsa he will greet him by saying, "Waheguru Ji Ka Khalsa, Waheguru Ji Ka Fateh" (the Khalsa belongs to God, Victory belongs to God).

The Sikh Gurus

The Sikh religion was developed by ten Gurus, beginning with Guru Nanak Dev.

Guru Nanak

The founder of the Sikh religion, Guru Nanak Dev, was born in 1469 in the western Punjab village of Talwandi. He was born into a Hindu family but his father worked for the local Muslim government.

At this time, India was run by Muslim rulers, and from an early age Guru Nanak was interested in both Hindu and Islamic ideas and faith.

One day when he was 30 years old, Guru Nanak went to bathe in the river and disappeared for three days. God had taken him into the river in order to show him God's word.

When he came out of the river, Guru Nanak gave up all of his possessions and began travelling around India, teaching the word of God. The first lesson that he taught was, "There is no Hindu, no Muslim." This meant that there is no difference between one person and another in God's eyes, everyone is equal, no matter what they believe.

After 25 years of travelling and preaching the ideas of Sikhism, Guru Nanak settled at Kartarpur. Before he died, Guru Nanak chose Angad Dev to be the next Sikh Guru.

The Sikh Gurus

Guru Angad Dev created a new way of writing the Punjabi language, called the **GURMUKI** script. This is the style of writing used to write the Guru Granth Sahib, the Sikh holy book.

Guru Amar Das was 70 years old when he became Guru. He did much to organise the Sikh society and faith and fought for the equality of women in all aspects of life.

Guru Ram Das established the city of Amritsar as the centre of Sikhism and was a great poet.

Guru Arjan Dev began the building of the **GOLDEN TEMPLE** at Amritsar and began compiling the Guru Granth Sahib. He often stood up for the poor when dealing with the government and worked hard to help the poor get their taxes lowered.

Guru Hargobind was only 11 when he became the sixth Guru. He recruited a Sikh army to protect the Sikhs and the poor of other faiths, and he built the Sikh administration building, the Akal Takht, in Amritsar.

Guru Har Rai, Guru Har Krishnan and Guru Tegh Bahadur all expanded the Sikh faith and helped the poor. Guru Bahadur was tortured and executed for refusing to convert to Islam.

Guru Gobind Singh started the Khalsa, and gave Sikhs the five Ks and the baptism ceremony. He also completed the Guru Granth Sahib. Before he died he told the Sikhs that after him, there would be no more living Gurus and that the Guru Granth Sahib would be Sikhism's only Guru.

◀ This picture shows all 10 Sikh Gurus. The largest picture is of Guru Nanak (1469–1539). Next to him is Guru Gobind Singh (1666–1708). On the second line, from left to right, is Guru Angad (1504–1552), the Guru Granth Sahib, Guru Har Krishnan (1656–1664), and Guru Tegh Bahadur (1621–1675). On the bottom line, from left to right, is Guru Amar Das (1479–1574), Guru Ram Das (1534–1581), Guru Arjan (1563–1606), Guru Hargobind (1595–1644) and Guru Har Rai (1630–1661).

Weblink: www.CurriculumVisions.com

▼ A close-up view of a khanga or comb. The man showing us the comb is also wearing a kara, or steel bracelet.

Sikhism in everyday life

As part of their beliefs, Khalsa (baptised) Sikhs carry symbols of their faith with them at all times.

All baptised Sikhs must wear certain items every day. These make Sikhs easily identifiable, and are important symbols of their faith and community.

After he created the baptism ceremony for the Khalsa, Guru Singh said that each member of the Khalsa should always wear five items, to remind them of their faith and their duty to the community. These are the **FIVE Ks**. They are called the five Ks because the name of each item begins with a K in the Punjabi language.

The five Ks

Kara

The word kara means a link or bond. The kara is a steel bracelet which stands for an unbreakable link or bond with the Guru Granth Sahib and with the community of Sikhs.

The kara is made of steel for two reasons. One is that many people cannot afford more valuable metals like gold and silver. So, the steel is a symbol of equality. Steel is also a symbol of physical, mental and moral strength.

The simple circular shape of the kara is a reminder that God has no beginning and no end, just like a circle, and is a symbol of the oneness of God.

Khanga

Khanga means comb. Baptised Sikhs wear a small wooden comb in their hair all the time. The comb is a symbol of cleanliness. Just as a comb helps remove tangles and cleans the hair, it is also a reminder to clean away any impure thoughts.

When Sikhism was founded, it was common for religious teachers to live as ASCETICS. These people had uncombed, matted hair. The neat, combed hair of the Sikhs is also a sign that they believe asceticism is not the correct path to God. Sikhs tie up their hair neatly and wash it every day.

▶ Necklace with khanga and a tiny kirpan.

▼ These Sikh men do not ever cut their hair or beards.

Kesh

Kesh means hair. A Sikh should treat hair as a gift from God. Because hair is an integral part of the human body, created by God, Khalsa Sikhs do not cut their hair. Uncut hair is a symbol of faith and confirms a Sikh's belief in the acceptance of God's Will.

▲ A type of kirpan. There are many different styles of kirpan.

Kaccha

Kaccha is a pair of shorts. This is special, slightly longer type of underwear that is a reminder of the need for self-restraint and preparedness. Because kaccha is long, it can be worn without causing embarrassment, and is a sign that the wearer is always ready to take action, for example, to jump in the water to save someone.

Kirpan

The word kirpan means sword. It comes from the words 'kirpa', meaning an act of kindness, and 'aan' meaning honour and self-respect. The kirpan stands for a readiness to defend the weak and fight for what is right. It is an emblem of courage, dignity and self-reliance. It is worn purely as a religious symbol and not as a weapon.

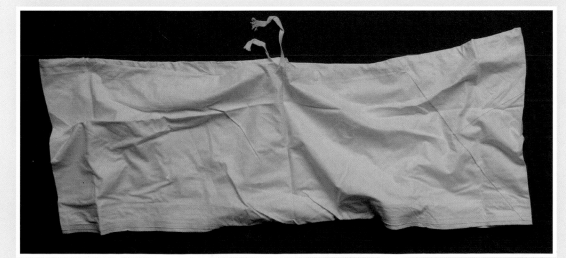

◄ When Sikhism began, most people did not wear fitted underwear. Instead they only wore a loose cloth. The kaccha are more modest.

◀ This young boy is wearing only an underturban.

▼ Under this man's turban, you can see two black cords, or straps. These are used to keep his long beard neat and out of the way (remember, baptised Sikhs cannot ever cut any of their hair).

The turban

The **TURBAN**, or dastaar, is an important part of Sikhism. When Sikhism was founded, the turban was a symbol of high status and royalty. After he introduced the baptism ceremony, Guru Gobind Singh made wearing a turban a requirement for all baptised Sikh men (it is optional for women, but many women choose to wear one).

At the first baptism ceremony, Guru Gobind Singh explained that all baptised Sikhs were royalty, and the turban was their crown.

Turbans are symbols of respect for God in many cultures, and this is true in Sikhism also. The turban also keeps long hair neat and tidy.

In today's society, it can be difficult to wear a turban all the time. For example, how can you wear a uniform or a bicycle helmet with a turban? But Sikhs have fought long and hard for their right to always wear the turban.

A Sikh turban can be any colour and there are many different ways to tie a turban. Each person ties their own turban. Underneath the turban is an underturban, or cap, called a **PATKA**. This keeps the hair in place while the turban is being tied. The patka is also useful when swimming or doing sports, where a full turban might get in the way.

▼ There are many different ways to tie a turban and different turban styles. Most boys learn to tie a turban even before they are baptised.

The Guru Granth Sahib

This is the Sikh holy book. It is always treated with great respect and contains hymns that were inspired by God.

All of the Sikh Gurus wrote hymns, poems and other writings in praise of God. Guru Arjan Dev, the fifth Guru, collected all of the writings of the first four Gurus and put them together into a book, the **ADI GRANTH**, or **GURU GRANTH SAHIB** (often called simply 'The Guru').

Later, Guru Gobind Singh completed the Guru Granth Sahib by collecting the writings of the rest of the Gurus and adding them to the book. Guru Singh placed the book in the **GOLDEN TEMPLE** and told the Sikhs that after his death, the Guru Granth Sahib would be the supreme spiritual authority and head of the Sikh religion, rather than any living person.

What is in the Guru

The Guru Granth Sahib not only contains the works of the ten Sikh Gurus, but also writings of people from other faiths, including Hindus,

▲ The Guru Granth Sahib is divided into 33 sections. The first section contains the epic Japji poem by Guru Nanak, which is not meant to be sung. The next 31 sections are the ragas, hymns, which are meant to be sung and accompanied by music. The last section is a collection of assorted verses by different authors.

Muslims and **SUFIS**. Some of the hymns were written by kings, princes or well-known poets from the time, but others were written by ordinary people, such as cobblers and butchers. Many of the hymns were also written by musicians.

Through listening to the hymns in the Guru Granth Sahib, and **MEDITATING** on their meaning, each person can be brought closer to God.

Guru Arjan once described the Guru like this: "In this dish are placed three things: Truth, Harmony and Wisdom. These are seasoned with the Name of God which is the basis of all; whoever eats it and relishes it, shall be saved."

◀ Anyone who can read the Gurmuki script is allowed to read the Guru during worship. The person doing the reading is called a GRANTHI. While it is being read, a CHAURI, usually made from yak hair, is waved over the book. This is the way royalty were treated in India at the time Sikhism was founded and is considered a sign of respect.

means 'the Guru's word' or 'song messages'. The hymns have been arranged according to the melody (RAGA) in which they are meant to be sung, by author and by the musical key in which they are sung.

Care of the Guru

When it is in the GURDWARA during worship, the Guru is placed on cushions on a platform called a TAKHT, which means 'throne'. Over the takht is a canopy. When it is not being read from, the Guru is covered with a cloth called a RUMALA. All of these are signs of respect.

The Guru Granth Sahib is treated similarly to how a living Guru would be treated.

For example, if a person needs spiritual guidance, they might open the Guru at random, read the first poem or hymn they find and then think about how what they have read might help them. Sikhs also treat the book with the same respect they would treat a living Guru.

The Guru Granth Sahib is exactly 1,430 pages in length. Most of the book is written in Punjabi, but some hymns use Persian, **SANSKRIT** and Arabic words. All of the hymns are written in the Punjabi script known as **GURMUKI**, created by Guru Angad Dev.

The hymns in the Guru Granth Sahib are called **GURBANI**, which

Weblink: www.CurriculumVisions.com

Sikh baptism

The baptism ceremony is one of the most important parts of Sikh worship.

The first baptism ceremony

On April 13, 1699, Guru Gobind Singh (the tenth Guru, 1666–1708) called all the Sikh leaders to the city of Anandpur, in Punjab. In front of the congregation, Guru Gobind appeared with a drawn sword and asked for a volunteer who was prepared to die for God. Eventually one devout Sikh volunteered. The Guru took him behind a screen, the crowd heard a thud, and the Guru came back out with his sword dripping with blood.

Four more men volunteered, and the same thing happened. Then, the Guru brought all five men out from behind the screen. They were alive through a miracle of God. It was a test to select the most loyal and devout Sikhs.

These five men are known as Panj Piares or the **FIVE BELOVED**. They were the first Sikhs to be initiated into the Khalsa community through the Amrit, or baptism ceremony. The Panj Piares then baptised the Guru.

The Amrit ceremony

Each Sikh chooses for themself when to go through the Amrit ceremony. It is usually done when a person is in their late teens, or when they are mature enough to accept the responsibility of being a member of the Khalsa.

The ceremony is performed by six members of the Khalsa. Before the ceremony, the person being baptised puts on the five Ks for the first time.

During the ceremony special hymns are sung and prayers are read. Amrit (specially prepared sugar water that has been stirred by a double-edged sword) is sprinkled on their eyes and hair, then they take a drink of the mixture.

▲ Five members of the Khalsa during a Sikh festival. They are symbolic of the Panj Piares or Five Beloved.

This is followed by an explanation of the code of conduct and discipline required for a Khalsa. Every member of the Khalsa is required to wear the five Ks and abstain from cutting their hair, eating **HALAL** meat, living with a member of the opposite sex without being married and using intoxicants such as tobacco and alcohol.

Other breaches of the code of conduct are also explained and the **ARDAS** prayer is read. This is followed by taking **HUKAM** (opening the Guru to a random page and reading the first hymn on that page) and eating **KARDH PARSHAD** (sacred pudding) from a common bowl.

The new member of the Khalsa is given the new surname of Singh (lion heart) if they are a man, and Kaur (princess) if they are a woman.

Worship

The main room inside a gurdwara is called the diwan hall. This is where worship takes place.

◀▼ Worship in the DIWAN HALL.
(Left) Men usually sit on the right and women on the left. There are no chairs in the diwan hall. This emphasises that everyone is equal.

(Main picture) The Guru Granth Sahib is placed on a small raised platform called the Manji Sahib. The Manji Sahib is covered with a nice cloth and is, in turn, placed on a larger platform (big enough to hold the Manji Sahib and the granthi), called the takht. The entire takht is covered by a canopy (PALKI).

When worshippers enter the diwan hall they first bow to the Guru, in order to show respect, then they leave an offering of food or money, which is used to help run the gurdwara.

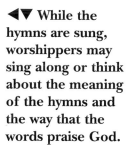

◀▼ While the hymns are sung, worshippers may sing along or think about the meaning of the hymns and the way that the words praise God.

While Sikhs often worship on their own, most Sikh worship takes place with others and in the presence of the Guru Granth Sahib in the **GURDWARA**. The word gurdwara means 'Gateway to the Guru'.

Worship alone

There are three daily prayers that can be said on your own. These are: Japu Sahib and four other hymns, said in the morning; Rehras, nine hymns written by the third, fifth and tenth Gurus, and recited in the evening; and Sohila (or Aarti), which is a prayer of thanksgiving said at bedtime. The **ARDAS** prayer is also said after any other prayer.

Another way for Sikhs to worship on their own is to meditate (sit and think quietly about God). This can be done any time.

Worship services

Group worship services take place in the gurdwara. Group worship is called **SANGAT**.

The gurdwara usually remains open throughout the day, so that worshippers can offer prayers at any time convenient to them. Outside India, gurdwaras may only be open for group worship on certain days or times. In India, two services are held daily in every gurdwara, one in the morning and the other in the evening.

In some gurdwaras worship services may take place all day, every day, and people come and go throughout the day for as much of the service as they can. The emphasis is on meditating (thinking) about God and so most of the service involves listening to readings from the Guru Granth Sahib and to hymns being sung from the Guru Granth Sahib, to accompanying music.

Music plays a very important part in worship at the gurdwara. Each of the hymns in the Guru Granth Sahib was written in a particular melody (raga) and rhythm (talas). The professional musicians (called ragis) who play in the gurdwara are trained in the styles that go with each hymn. In the absence of any trained musicians, the congregation sings the hymns in chorus.

Daily worship services

In the morning a prayer called Asa-di-Var is sung or recited, followed by the Anand Sahib, the Ardas prayer and a hukam (opening the Guru to a random page and reading the first hymn on that page), then follows the distribution of kardh parshad (sacred food).

In the evening, prayers called Rehras and Chaupai are recited by the granthi (reader of the scripture) or by the sangat (congregation).

Then hymns are sung by the ragis or recited by the sangat. After Ardas and hukam, kardh parshad is distributed. Finally, the Guru Granth Sahib is ceremoniously wrapped up and taken to a special room for the night.

On some days there may also be a sermon or a talk, given by a member of the congregation or a visitor.

▼ There is no priesthood in Sikhism. In a large gurdwara, someone may be employed to be a full-time granthi. In a smaller gurdwara, members of the congregation will take turns to be granthi.

▶ Sacred music is called KIRTAN, meaning 'singing the praises of God'. Generally in the gurdwara, musicians, called ragis, either sing alone or request the sangat to repeat after them the lines of the hymn in chorus. The Sikh Gurus composed hymns to be sung according to certain musical rhythms (called ragas). There are 31 different ragas. Traditional instruments like the tabla (drums) and harmonium (a type of piano) are most commonly used, but more modern instruments, like guitars, can also be used.

In the gurdwara

Sikhs generally bathe before going to the gurdwara. They take off their shoes at the gate. When they enter the main hall, they kneel down and bow before the Guru Granth Sahib, they also make an offering in cash or food for the LANGAR. Everyone must cover their heads as a sign of respect.

▼ After worship, each member of the congregation is given kardh parshad, or sacred pudding. This is a sweet made from cooking together equal amounts of clarified butter, wheat flour and sugar while certain prayers are recited. Members of the congregation usually take turns to make the pudding.

The langar

The langar is a community kitchen which is run by volunteers. It is a part of worship, but also a type of charity.

▲ These women are all volunteers. They are making bread for the langar. This may look like a lot of dough, but a large gurdwara will feed thousands of people each day.

Guru Nanak taught that all Sikhs should share what they have with others. This principle of Sikhism can be seen in the hymn Var Sarang: "Save, eat and give away something, such a person finds the path."

History of the langar

Almost everyone who visited Guru Nanak brought gifts, often of food. At first, Guru Nanak gave these gifts away to the poor, but as more and more people began visiting, Guru Nanak decided to start up a free kitchen, called a **LANGAR**, to distribute food to the poor. At the same time,

he began the practice of having all worshippers share a meal, called **PANGAT**, as a part of worship. Guru Nanak insisted that before anyone could see him, they had to eat in the langar. Thus, for Sikhs, eating in the langar is a form of worship.

Equality in the langar

Everyone is welcome to eat in the langar. In the langar everyone, rich and poor, Sikh and non-Sikh, eats together. All the food is **VEGETARIAN**.

▼ Any type of food may be served in the langar, but it is always vegetarian. This is because people of all religions are welcome to eat in the langar. Some religions have restrictions on what they can eat, but everyone can eat vegetarian food.

▲ In the langar, everyone eats sitting in a row. This is a way of demonstrating that all people are equal.

Everyone eats the same food and sits all in a row on the floor, so no one is in front of or higher than anyone else. Thus, everyone who eats in the langar takes part in one of the highest Sikh ideals – equality. This can be seen in the following story.

One of Guru Hargobind's disciples was Jhanda, a rich man. One day the Guru asked his disciples to fetch fuel wood from the jungle for the langar. Jhanda was gone for two days and Guru Hargobind became worried about him. Finally, Jhanda was seen coming from the jungle with a bundle of firewood on his back. Guru Hargobind told Jhanda that he should not have undertaken such a menial job. Jhanda replied that the Guru had asked Sikhs to fetch wood. He was a Sikh and so he went to the jungle. As he was not used to breaking wood, it took him time to collect it. Even though he was rich, Jhanda was willing to do menial work.

Similarly, every Sikh is expected to contribute to the langar, either by giving food or money, or by working in the langar, cooking, serving and cleaning. Often, Sikhs say prayers or hymns while working in the langar, or use the time to think about the meaning of service (seva).

Today, every gurdwara has a langar attached to it. The langar acts as a free kitchen for the hungry and also a form of worship for the Sikh community.

Sikh symbols

There are some symbols which have special meaning to Sikhs.

The Sikh flag – nishan sahib

The Sikh flag is a saffron-coloured, triangular-shaped cloth, usually with the KHANDA symbol on it in blue. It is usually mounted on a long steel pole (which is also covered with saffron-coloured cloth). Every gurdwara has a Sikh flag flying outside.

Sikhs show great respect to their flag as it is, indeed, the symbol of the freedom of the Khalsa.

▼ The Sikh flag is a proud symbol of Sikhism. It is flown outside every gurdwara, so it also tells people where to find a gurdwara. On holidays, when the Guru is paraded through the streets, it is a special honour to carry the Sikh flag in the procession.

The following story shows the importance that Sikhs place on the flag: Once, a flag bearer named Bhai Alam Singh fell in the hands of enemy forces during a battle. He was told to throw away the flag or else his hands would be chopped off. Bhai Alam replied that in that case he would keep holding the flag with his feet. He was then told that his feet would also be cut off.

Bhai Alam replied that he would hold it with his mouth. "Your head will be cut off, then what will you do?" he was asked. Bhai Alam Singh replied with confidence, "The Guru whose flag I am carrying will take care of it."

The Golden Temple

The GOLDEN TEMPLE in Amritsar, India, also called the Harimandir, is a living symbol of the spiritual and historical traditions of the Sikhs. Today, it is the home and the centre of the Sikh faith.

The temple was founded by Guru Amar Das, but it is located on a site which was thought to be holy for thousands of years and for many different religions. The original copy of the Guru Granth Sahib was placed in this gurdwara.

Next to the temple is a building which serves as the administrative centre for Sikhism, the Akal Takht.

The Sikh insignia – khanda

The khanda is three symbols in one. The name comes from the double-edged sword, called a khanda, in the centre of the symbol. The sword symbolises God's ability to distinguish truth from falsehood. A khanda sword was used by Guru Gobind Singh to prepare the amrit for the first baptism ceremony.

The khanda sword is surrounded by a circular iron weapon called a chakka, which represents the oneness of God. Around the circle are two longer swords which stand for spiritual and worldly power.

These words are IK ONKAR, meaning 'There is only one God'. They are the first two words of the Guru Granth Sahib.

The right edge of the double-edged khanda sword stands for freedom and authority.

The left edge represents divine justice.

Sikh ceremonies and holidays

Most Sikh festivals and holidays commemorate important events in Sikh history.

Sikhs do not believe in empty rituals or ceremonies. So, all Sikh ceremonies and festivals are primarily about showing devotion to God.

All the Sikh ceremonies like birth, baptism, marriage and death are simple, inexpensive and have a religious tone. They are held in the presence of the Guru Granth Sahib and include kirtan, the singing of appropriate hymns for the occasion, saying of Ardas – a formal prayer, and the distribution of kardh parshad, sacred food, to the congregation. Many Sikhs also commemorate important events in their lives with a ceremony called an **AKHAND PATH**.

Akhand path

An akhand path is the reading of the entire Guru Granth Sahib, with no breaks. This usually takes 48 hours and several different people take turns reading.

Akhand paths marking important dates in the Sikh calendar are performed at the gurdwara, whereas those marking personal family events are normally performed at home.

▲▶ In the picture *(right)* you can just see the top of the pink palanquin carrying the Guru Granth Sahib. Most of the people are following along in the procession. The picture *(above)* shows a granthi on the float, waving a chauri over the Guru. The chauri is a traditional symbol of authority.

Nagar kirtan

The **NAGAR KIRTAN** is used to mark holidays and important events in Sikh history. During the nagar kirtan, the Guru Granth Sahib is taken out of the gurdwara, placed in a special **PALANQUIN** and paraded around the neighbourhood.

▲ At the front of the nagar kirtan procession, people sweep the streets for the men carrying the Sikh flag, who are bare-footed.

◄ This picture shows a group of Sikh musicians playing and singing hymns during a nagar kirtan procession. The 'float' containing the Guru Granth Sahib has already passed by, and following behind it is this 'float', which is made up of a flat-bed truck, which has been decorated with cushions and posters for this procession.

The man on the right side of the photo is playing a traditional type of Indian drum called a tabla. The woman in the middle is playing a modern version of another traditional instrument, called a harmonium. Most of the other people in the truck are singing hymns from the Guru Granth Sahib. You can see that some of them have microphones so they can be heard by the large crowd.

The Guru is accompanied by many people and often by other 'floats'. During the procession, hymns are sung, music is played and the Guru may be read out loud.

Gurupurabs

GURUPURABS are anniversaries associated with the lives of the Sikh Gurus. Sikhs celebrate ten gurupurabs in a year. At each of these festivals, one of the ten Gurus is honoured.

Guru Nanak's gurupurab falls in the month of Kartik (October/November). The Sikhs believe that Guru Nanak brought enlightenment to the world, so his gurupurab is also called Prakash Utsav, the festival of light.

Gurupurabs are celebrated in the gurdwara with an akhand path.

On the day of the festival there is a nagar kirtan. Five armed guards, who represent the Panj Piares, head the procession, each carrying a Sikh flag (nishan sahib).

Sweets and community lunches are also offered to everyone in an outdoor langar. Sikhs visit gurdwaras where special programmes are arranged and hymns are sung.

Baisakh

Baisakh is New Year's Day in Punjab. It falls in the month of Vaisakh (April/May). It was on this day that the tenth Sikh Guru, Guru Gobind Singh, founded the Khalsa (the Sikh brotherhood) in 1699.

To commemorate this event, special worship services are held in the gurdwara. The main celebration however, takes place in the gurdwara at Anandpur, in the Punjab, where the Khalsa was first formed.

The Guru Granth Sahib is ceremonially taken out, symbolically bathed with milk and water and placed on its throne. Granthi chant the verses that were recited by the original Panj Piares when the Khalsa was created. While these are being chanted, amrit is prepared in an iron vessel and distributed. Worshippers sip the amrit five times and vow to work for the good of the Sikh community.

▼ This picture shows an outdoor langar, which is common during Sikh festivals and nagar kirtan. In the bottom left of the photo, you can see a man with a cup of chai (sweet, spiced milk tea). The man on the right is handing out bags of food. All along the route of the nagar kirtan, worshippers from the gurdwara are handing out free food and drink.

Non-Sikhs are always welcome to follow along with the procession and to share in the outdoor langar.

Diwali

The Hindu festival of Diwali coincides with the Sikh celebration of the return of Guru Hargobind from imprisonment. The Sikhs celebrate this day as Bandi Chhorh Divas, 'the day of release of detainees'.

In 1619, Emperor Jahangir, the emperor of India, had imprisoned Guru Hargobind and 60 other rajahs in the Gwalior Fort. The Emperor was under pressure from the Guru's Muslim friends to release him and finally agreed.

According to Sikh tradition, the Guru agreed to be freed only if the other rajahs imprisoned with him were freed. The Emperor did not want to agree, but he finally said, "Let those rajahs be freed who can hold on to the Guru's coat tails and walk out of prison". He thought only four or five would be able to do this. However, Guru Hargobind made a special coat with 52 coat tails – and so all the rajahs were freed.

Today, Sikhs celebrate this festival by lighting lamps and fireworks and saying prayers in the gurdwara.

Weblink: www.CurriculumVisions.com

Glossary

ADI GRANTH Adi means first, Adi Granth is the first edition of the Guru Granth Sahib as compiled by Guru Arjan Dev in 1604.

AKHAND PATH An uninterrupted continuous reading of the Guru Granth Sahib. It is undertaken by a team of readers and takes approximately 48 hours.

AMRIT The word amrit means nectar. It is sugar water which is used during the Khalsa baptism ceremony. Amrit is also the name of the ceremony.

ARDAS An important Sikh prayer recited at the conclusion of a service. The word ardas means supplication (to pray).

ASCETIC A person who attempts to find salvation by giving up all comforts and living away from all family, friends and distractions.

BAPTISM In Sikhism, this is a ceremony where a person accepts certain responsibilities and agrees to live by Sikh guidelines and rules.

CASTE A way of organising society that was common in India. In a caste society each person is born into a certain station (caste) in life and cannot rise above it.

CHAURI A fly whisk. The chauri is an ancient symbol of royalty in India. Rulers and kings would have someone waving a chauri over them at all times. It is usually made of yak hair or peacock feathers and is waved over the Guru Granth Sahib whenever it is open.

DIWAN HALL The room in a gurdwara where religious services take place. The word diwan means congregational worship where the Guru Granth Sahib is present.

FIVE BELOVED The first five members of the Khalsa. Each of them volunteered to sacrifice their life for Sikhism.

FIVE KS (5KS) Five symbols of Sikhism that every baptised Sikh must wear. *See* kaccha, kara, kesh, khanga, kirpan.

GOLDEN TEMPLE also called the Harimandir. This is the main Sikh gurdwara in Amritsar, India, and the centre of the Sikh faith.

GRANTHI A custodian of the Guru Granth Sahib. Any baptised Sikh can be a granthi. The granthi reads from the Guru Granth Sahib during worship service in the gurdwara.

GURBANI All of the writings of the Gurus.

GURDWARA The name given to a Sikh temple. It means 'doorway to the house of God'. Any building that contains a copy of the Guru Granth Sahib may be a gurdwara.

GURMUKI Sikh script. Gurmuki is a way of writing the Punjabi language. It was developed by Guru Angad Dev as a way to make reading Punjabi easier for ordinary people.

GURU A word meaning teacher, which usually refers to a spiritual or religious teacher. In Sikhism, the ten founders of the Sikh faith are referred to as Gurus. Also, the Guru Granth Sahib is sometimes called, simply, The Guru.

GURU GRANTH SAHIB The holy book of the Sikh faith. It contains hymns written by many different people, but each one was inspired directly by God.

GURU NANAK DEV The founder of Sikhism.

GURUPURAB The celebration of the anniversary of the birth or death of a Guru. Also applied to the anniversary of the installation of the Guru Granth Sahib in the Golden Temple in 1604 or the deaths of the sons of Guru Gobind Singh.

HALAL Something lawful or permitted in Islam.

HUKAM When the Guru Granth Sahib is opened to a random page and the first hymn on the page is read aloud as the 'lesson' for the day. This is called 'taking hukam' or hukamnama. The word hukam means 'instructions'. Sikhs may also take hukam when they are in need of advice.

IK ONKAR The first two words of the Guru Granth Sahib. They mean 'God is one'. The words ik onkar, written in the Gurmuki script, are also used as a Sikh symbol.

KACCHA Modest underwear. One of the five Ks and a symbol of self-control.

KARA A steel bracelet. One of the five Ks and a symbol of restraint and the oneness of God.

KARDH PARSHAD A sweet served at religious ceremonies in the presence of the Guru Granth Sahib and sanctified by prayers. It is a symbol of equality of all members of the congregation.

KESH (or kes) Uncut hair. One of the five Ks and a symbol of spirituality.

KHALSA The name for the worldwide group of all baptised Sikhs.

KHANDA A Sikh symbol. It consists of three parts: a double-edged sword, also called the khanda, a circular iron weapon called a chakka, and two longer swords.

KHANGA A comb. One of the five Ks and a symbol of hygiene and discipline.

KIRPAN A sword. One of the five Ks and a symbol of the Sikh fight against injustice and religious oppression.

KIRTAN Singing the hymns in the Guru Granth Sahib, accompanied by music.

LANGAR Free community kitchen found in all Sikh gurdwaras. For Sikhs, eating and working in the langar is a form of worship. The langar is open to anyone, and is also an important symbol of equality.

MEDITATE/MEDITATION A way of sitting and thinking about God.

NAGAR KIRTAN A procession where the Guru Granth Sahib is paraded around the neighbourhood of the gurdwara. It often takes place on holidays like gurupurabs.

PALANQUIN A special throne or seat.

PALKI The palanquin or seat on which the Guru Granth Sahib is ceremonially installed.

PANGAT This is the meal that the congregation eats together in the langar. It is different from when a non-Sikh eats in the langar in that it is part of Sikh worship.

PANJ PIARES *See* Five Beloved

PATKA An underturban worn underneath the turban to keep the hair tidy. It can also be worn instead of a turban during sports or at other times.

PUNJAB A region of India and Pakistan where Sikhism began.

PUNJABI The main language of the people of Punjab.

RAGA A tune. In Sikhism, it is a tune designed to be used when singing sacred hymns.

REHT MARYADA The Sikh code of conduct. It was not created by the Gurus, but by a committee after the time of the Gurus.

REINCARNATION The idea that when we die, our soul is reborn into a different body.

RUMALA The cloth which is used ceremonially to cover the Guru Granth Sahib.

SANGAT The Sikh congregation during worship.

SANSKRIT An ancient language used in India. Many ancient Asian holy books are written in Sanskrit.

SIKH A person who follows the Sikh faith.

SUFI A person who follows the mystical branch of Islam, called Sufism.

TAKHT The platform in the diwan hall where the Guru Granth Sahib is placed during worship. Takht is also the name of the five gurdwaras that serve as the administrative centres for the Sikh faith. The most important of these is the Akal Takht, in Amritsar.

TURBAN A head covering consisting of a long cloth wound around the head. Turbans are worn in many cultures around the world and for many different reasons. For Sikhs, the turban is an important symbol of their religion and beliefs.

VEGETARIAN A person who does not eat any meat.

WAHEGURU Meaning 'the wonderful Lord' or 'true teacher'; it is the most popular Sikh name for God.

Index

Curriculum Visions is a registered trademark of Atlantic Europe Publishing Company Ltd.

Dedicated Web Site
There's more about other great Curriculum Visions packs and a wealth of supporting information available at our dedicated web site:

www.CurriculumVisions.com

First published in 2005 by
Atlantic Europe Publishing Company Ltd
Copyright © 2005
Atlantic Europe Publishing Company Ltd

All rights reserved. No part of this publication may be reproduced, stored in a retrieval system, or transmitted in any form or by any means, electronic, mechanical, photocopying, recording or otherwise, without prior permission of the Publisher.

Authors
Lisa Magloff, MA and Brian Knapp, BSc, PhD

Religious Adviser
Hardeep Singh

Art Director
Duncan McCrae, BSc

Senior Designer
Adele Humphries, BA

Acknowledgements
The publishers would like to thank the following for their help and advice:
Sri Guru Singh Sabha Gurdwara, and the Sikh community of Southall, London.

Photographs
The Earthscape Editions photolibrary, except pages 8–9 Art Directors/TRIP.

Illustration
David Woodroffe

Designed and produced by
Earthscape Editions

Printed in China by
WKT Company Ltd

Sikh faith and practice
– Curriculum Visions
A CIP record for this book is available from the British Library

Paperback ISBN 1 86214 470 2
Hardback ISBN 1 86214 471 0

This product is manufactured from sustainable managed forests. For every tree cut down at least one more is planted.